Hal•Leonard®
Piano Play-Along

AUDIO
ACCESS
INCLUDED

PRIDE&PREJUDICE
MUSIC FROM THE MOTION PICTURE SOUNDTRACK

PLAYBACK+
Speed • Pitch • Balance • Loop

To access audio visit:
www.halleonard.com/mylibrary

8427-9451-9678-2355

ISBN 978-1-4234-7347-3

Hal•Leonard®
CORPORATION
7777 W. BLUEMOUND RD. P.O. BOX 13819 MILWAUKEE, WI 53213

Visit Hal Leonard Online at
www.halleonard.com

CONTENTS

ARRIVAL AT NETHERFIELD

By DARIO MARIANELLI

Moderately

With pedal throughout

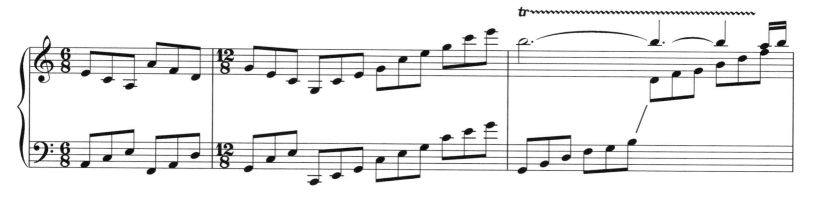

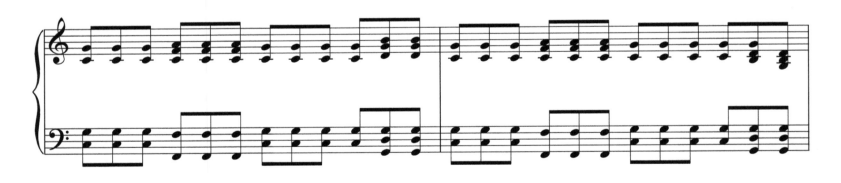

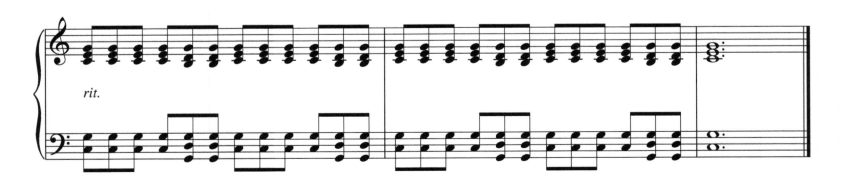

DAWN

By DARIO MARIANELLI

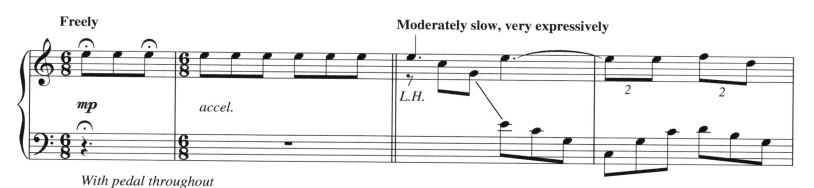

With pedal throughout

Moderately fast, with motion

Slightly slower

DARCY'S LETTER

By DARIO MARIANELLI

Quasi improvisando

With pedal throughout

16

GEORGIANA

By DARIO MARIANELLI

Moderately fast, in 4

mp - mf

LEAVING NETHERFIELD

By DARIO MARIANELLI

THE LIVING SCULPTURES OF PEMBERLEY

By DARIO MARIANELLI

MERYTON TOWNHALL

By HENRY PURCELL
Adapted and Arranged by DARIO MARIANELLI
and WILLIAM LYONS

Moderately fast, in 2

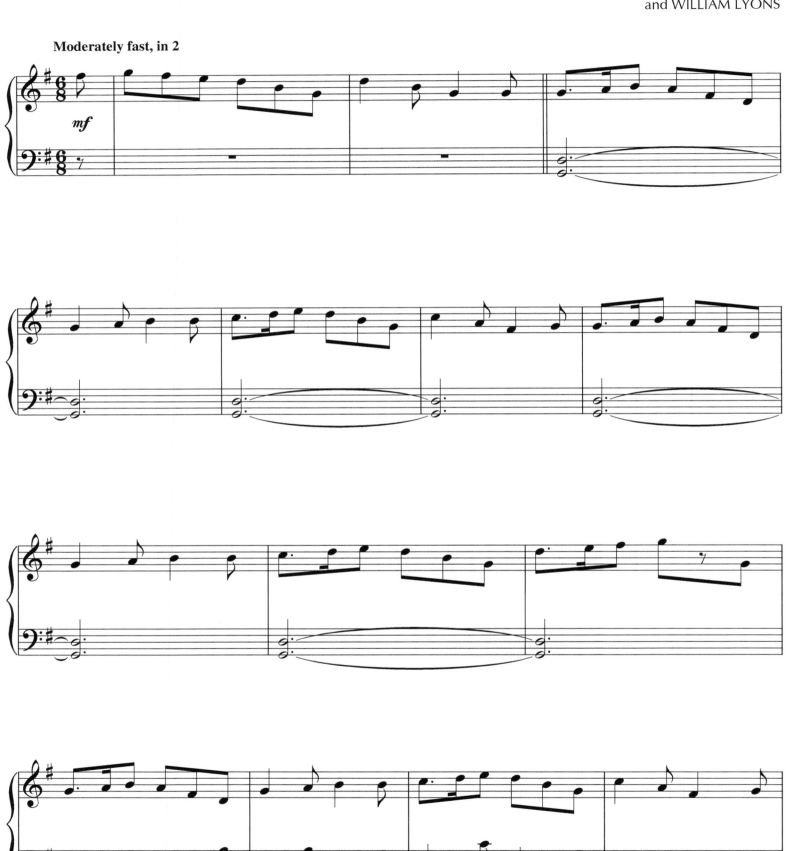

THE SECRET LIFE OF DAYDREAMS

By DARIO MARIANELLI

THE ULTIMATE SONGBOOKS

HAL·LEONARD® PIANO PLAY-ALONG

These great songbook/audio packs come with our standard arrangements for piano and voice with guitar chord frames plus audio. The audio includes a full performance of each song, as well as a second track without the piano part so you can play "lead" with the band!

BOOK/CD PACKS

1. **Movie Music** 00311072 .... $14.95
7. **Love Songs** 00311078 .... $14.95
12. **Christmas Favorites** 00311137 ....$15.95
15. **Favorite Standards** 00311146 .... $14.95
27. **Andrew Lloyd Webber Greats** 00311179 ..... $14.95
28. **Lennon & McCartney** 00311180 .... $14.95
44. **Frank Sinatra – Popular Hits** 00311277 .... $14.95
71. **George Gershwin** 00102687 .... $24.99
77. **Elton John Favorites** 00311884 .... $14.99
78. **Eric Clapton** 00311885 .... $14.99
81. **Josh Groban** 00311901 .... $14.99
82. **Lionel Richie** 00311902 .... $14.99
86. **Barry Manilow** 00311935 .... $14.99
87. **Patsy Cline** 00311936 .... $14.99
90. **Irish Favorites** 00311969 .... $14.99
92. **Disney Favorites** 00311973 .... $14.99
97. **Great Classical Themes** 00312020 .... $14.99
98. **Christmas Cheer** 00312021 .... $14.99
105. **Bee Gees** 00312055 .... $14.99
106. **Carole King** 00312056 .... $14.99
107. **Bob Dylan** 00312057 .... $16.99
108. **Simon & Garfunkel** 00312058 .... $16.99
114. **Motown** 00312176 .... $14.99
115. **John Denver** 00312249 .... $14.99
123. **Chris Tomlin** 00312563 .... $14.99
125. **Katy Perry** 00109373 .... $14.99

BOOKS/ONLINE AUDIO

5. **Disney** 00311076 .... $14.99
8. **The Piano Guys – Uncharted** 00202549 .... $24.99
9. **The Piano Guys – Christmas Together**
00259567 .... $24.99
16. **Coldplay** 00316506 .... $17.99
20. **La La Land** 00241591 .... $19.99
24. **Les Misérables** 00311169 .... $14.99
25. **The Sound of Music** 00311175 ....$15.99
30. **Elton John Hits** 00311182 ....$17.99
31. **Carpenters** 00311183 ....$17.99
32. **Adele** 00156222 .... $24.99
33. **Peanuts™** 00311227 ....$17.99
34. **A Charlie Brown Christmas** 00311228 .... $16.99
46. **Wicked** 00311317 ....$17.99
62. **Billy Joel Hits** 00311465 .... $14.99
65. **Casting Crowns** 00311494 .... $14.99
69. **Pirates of the Caribbean** 00311807 ....$17.99
72. **Van Morrison** 00103053 .... $16.99
73. **Mamma Mia! – The Movie** 00311831 ....$17.99
76. **Pride & Prejudice** 00311862 ....$15.99
83. **Phantom of the Opera** 00311903 .... $16.99
113. **Queen** 00312164 .... $16.99
117. **Alicia Keys** 00312306 ....$17.99
126. **Bruno Mars** 00123121 .... $19.99
127. **Star Wars** 00110282 .... $16.99
128. **Frozen** 00126480 .... $16.99
130. **West Side Story** 00130738 .... $14.99
131. **The Piano Guys – Wonders**
00141503 (Contains backing tracks only)....... $24.99